I0424708

TABLE OF CONTENTS

MP3 PLAYER
User manual

Important things to download

7Zip
(You only need to download this if you want to download the amv converter.) Although you may want it anyways as larger files downloaded from the internet are often compressed and need ZIP software to unpack them. Usually these programs cost upwards of $30-$40 The program below is tested free of viruses.

http://www.7-zip.org/

AMV Converter 4.0
http://www.frenzygear.com/thankyou.htm

IMPORTANT - PLEASE READ:

The ON/OFF SWITCH located on top of the device should normally be in the ON POSITION. Especially when charging. Turning the device off with the ON/OFF switch will shut it down completely and will take longer to turn on. You can also turn the device ON/OFF with the CENTER BUTTON just PRESS and HOLD. (ON/OFF SWITCH must be in the ON POSITION.)

If you are not actively using your device it may turn itself off,

(unless your settings are set to 0)

To turn it back on ensure the ON/OFF switch is in the ON position, PRESS/HOLD the CENTER button.

CHARGING: The ON/OFF SWITCH must be in the ON position while CHARGING. Connect the USB cord from your MP3 PLAYER to your WALL CHARGER, or COMPUTER.

(While learning to use your new device, we recommend plugging it into your computer. This way if you are reading the instructions and the device enters sleep mode or turns itself off, you can wake it up faster.)

The Main Menu is where you can choose between 9 options. **Music, Movie, Voice Recording, Voice Playback, FM radio, Photo, SET-UP, E-book, Games**. Use the arrow keys to scroll over to your selection . The press the Menu button to select your choice.

VOLUME -Press the VOLUME button, then press FF/VOL+ or RW/VOL- button to adjust volume accordingly, then press the VOL BUTTON again when you are finished.

IMPORTANT: Your media player is designed to power off the backlight when it is not actively being used. This is to save power. If you wish to extend the amount of time it takes until the backlight goes out while learning to use your player then see the section titled **SET-UP**.   We recommend changing it back to 10 seconds once you are comfortable with your player.

NEVER SET the DARKMODE to 0 as it will greatly reduce the battery life.

WE STRONGLY SUGGEST NOT TO UPGRADE THE FIRMWARE.

An incorrect firmware upgrade is difficult or impossible to undo, and will likely involve dismantling the device and shorting the memory to put it into 'recovery mode'. It is generally considered a bad idea to attempt a firmware upgrade as the benefit is likely negligible and one risks ruining the player software. Plus your warranty will not cover you.

SET UP

1)   Turn Player on

2)   Use the arrow keys to find SET UP

3)   Press MENU to select SET UP

You will now have the following options: Display Style, System time, LCD set, Language, Power off, Replay Mode, Online Mode, Memory Info, Firmware Version, Firmware upgrade (not recommended) EXIT. Use the arrow keys to scroll to your desired selection, then press the MENU button to select.

SYSTEM TIME – Scroll to SYSTEM TIME then Press MENU to select.

Now PRESS the CENTER BUTTON (The year should be highlighted.)

Press the arrow keys to change the year, PRESS the CENTER BUTTON to move on to Month/Day/Hour/Minutes/seconds. When finished press the MENU BUTTON to return to SET UP or hold the MENU BUTTON to return to MAIN MENU.

then press MENU again to save.

We recommend these settings

(This is to ensure your battery will last as long as possible…and to make it less annoying…especially when trying to learn how to use your device… if you do not adjust these settings, your battery may only last 1 hour and will keep shutting off on you.)

LCD set/DARKMODE-------- SET TO 30

Power off/ Off Time----------SET TO 0

SLEEP TIME ----------------------SET TO 0

Using your MP3 PLAYER to play MUSIC.

Ensure the ON/OFF switch is in the ON position. (Located on the top of the player) If the player was left in the ON position and is in sleep mode, you can press/hold the CENTER button to wake it up.

Use the ARROW keys to find MUSIC in the Main Menu. Then press MENU to select.

The music will be paused.

PLAY MUSIC - Press the CENTER PLAY/PAUSE button to play the music

OR press the MENU button to access LOCAL FOLDER (MUSIC LIBRARY), or to DELETE MUSIC FILES.

FF/RW - PRESS and HOLD FF or RW Button for a few seconds then let go. To instantly stop FF press the RW button. To instantly stop RW press the FF button.

NEXT SONG/PREVIOUS SONG – Press FF/RW button.

VOLUME – WHILE PLAYING MUSIC Press the VOLUME button then press FF/VOL+ or RW/VOL- button to adjust volume accordingly, then press the VOL BUTTON again when you are finished.

To access REPEAT-EQUALIZER-TEMPO RATE-REPLAY-REPLAY TIMES-REPLAY GAP

Press MENU button while MUSIC IS PLAYING.

RETURN TO MAIN MENU – PRESS and HOLD "MENU" Button.

You can use several different software programs to use with your MP3 PLAYER for converting music from most formats to MP3 or WMA.

(MP3 is better quality than WMA-however WMA sounds great to me and takes up less space than MP3)

I recommend using Windows Media Player.

(Windows Media Player is the easiest software to use for downloading music from the internet or converting your cd collection for use with your MP3 PLAYER.)

To Download WINDOWS MEDIA PLAYER click on this link below.

http://www.microsoft.com/windows/windowsmedia

FOR HELP USING WINDOWS MEDIA PLAYER CLICK ON THE LINKS BELOW

http://www.microsoft.com/windows/windowsmedia/player/faq/default.mspx

http://windowshelp.microsoft.com/Windows/en-US/Help/678d9218-a8d6-4b97-8c12-cec52a808a601033.mspx#EYB

Sites to download music.

What is the difference between eMusic and other digital music services?: eMusic stands alone as the only digital music service 100% that is focused on serving the needs of independent music fans and independent labels. eMusic is among the top digital music services, offering a diverse catalog of over 2 million tracks from established and emerging artists in every genre.

Q: How do I add eMusic downloads to my MP3 player?

A: First, make sure you have the eMusic Download Manager installed. The eMusic Download Manager makes downloading from eMusic a snap and will help organize your downloads. Check to make sure you have a folder labeled "My eMusic" on your computer's desktop. If you do, you're all set. If you do not, you will need to download and install the eMusic Download Manager by double-clicking on the file you downloaded.

http://musicmatch.com/

http://downloads.walmart.com/swap/

http://www.buy.com/buymusic/18250.html

http://www.apple.com/itunes/

Before downloading music from itunes be aware that you will have to burn the music to disk and reload to get rid of the "protected aac" format. Please read below for more information.

**Follow these directions to set up your device with iTunes for the first time.**

(Not recommended-Much more of a hassle than using Windows Media Player)

You must rename your device "FRENZY"

To do so go to the Start menu on your computer, then click on "my computer", now find the drive your device is connected to, "right click" rename…Frenzy

Download and install itunes http://www.apple.com/itunes/overview/

and the itunes agent http://ita.sourceforge.net/download.html to your computer.

IMPORTANT: **iTunes Agent** MUST BE INSTALLED in order for your MP4 player to work with iTunes. Click on the links above to download now.

Start iTunes Agent: If you receive an error asking for you to install v2.0.50727 then you can click on the link below to download it for free.

http://www.microsoft.com/downloads/details.aspx?FamilyID=0856eacb-4362-4b0d-8edd-aab15c5e04f5&DisplayLang=en

OPEN your iTunes Agent

PLUG YOUR MP3 PLAYER INTO THE USB PORT USING THE USB CABLE NOW.

In your system tray (bottom right corner of your screen) RIGHT CLICK on the iTunes Agent logo, then select PREFERENCES.

Click NEW

Under Device Information enter the following:

Name: FRENZY

Synchronize pattern: iTunes

Music folder: Music - **Click on the browse button, Select MY COMPUTER, then select FRENZY, then select MUSIC. (If you do not have a folder on your device named Music, you will need to create one.)**

Recognize by folder/file: Music

Associate with playlist: Use device name…

You're iTunes Agent is now set up – please close it now.

OPEN ITUNES

At the top menu click EDIT, Then select PREFERENCES, then select ADVANCED. Now click on the IMPORTING tab, and change the following:

Import using: MP3 Encoder

You are now set up to use iTunes with your MP3 PLAYER. – Please close your iTunes now.

USING iTunes

(Please read "SETTING UP YOUR MP3 PLAYER With iTunes" above)

Now that you've set iTunes up to work with your MP3 PLAYER **lets give it a try!** _

Open iTunes and your iTunes Agent

Import your music collection to itunes.

After the songs are imported to your iTunes, click on MUSIC (iTunes Library), select all of the songs in the folder that need to be converted to mp3 format, RIGHT CLICK, then select "convert selection to mp3"

After the songs are converted, transfer them to your FRENZY folder (right click/add to playlist/frenzy). You are now ready to synchronize the songs to your MP3 PLAYER.

When you are ready to synchronize your playlist to your MP3 PLAYER right click on the iTunes Agent in your system tray and select Synchronize Devices…

(If you receive a NO DEVICE CONNECTED message, try unplugging the MP3 PLAYER and plugging it back in again.) If that does not work, on YOUR COMPUTER click START/MY COMPUTER/ Now find the drive your device is connected to, and DOUBLE CLICK on it…when it opens ensure there is a file named MUSIC, if not the create another folder and name it MUSIC.

ALL SONGS DOWNLOADED FROM THE ITUNES MUSIC STORE IS IN PROTECTED AAC FORMAT! AND MUST BE BURNED TO DISK AND RELOADED TO GET RID OF THE DRM.

1. The first thing you need to do is to get rid of the "DRM" or in other words, unprotect your songs. This is not so that you can share them with your friends… that is illegal… this is only so that you can play your songs that you purchased thru the itunes music store on an mp3 player other than the apple ipod. First to find all of the songs that you purchased thru the itunes music store, click on the PURCHASED button on the left hand of the screen.

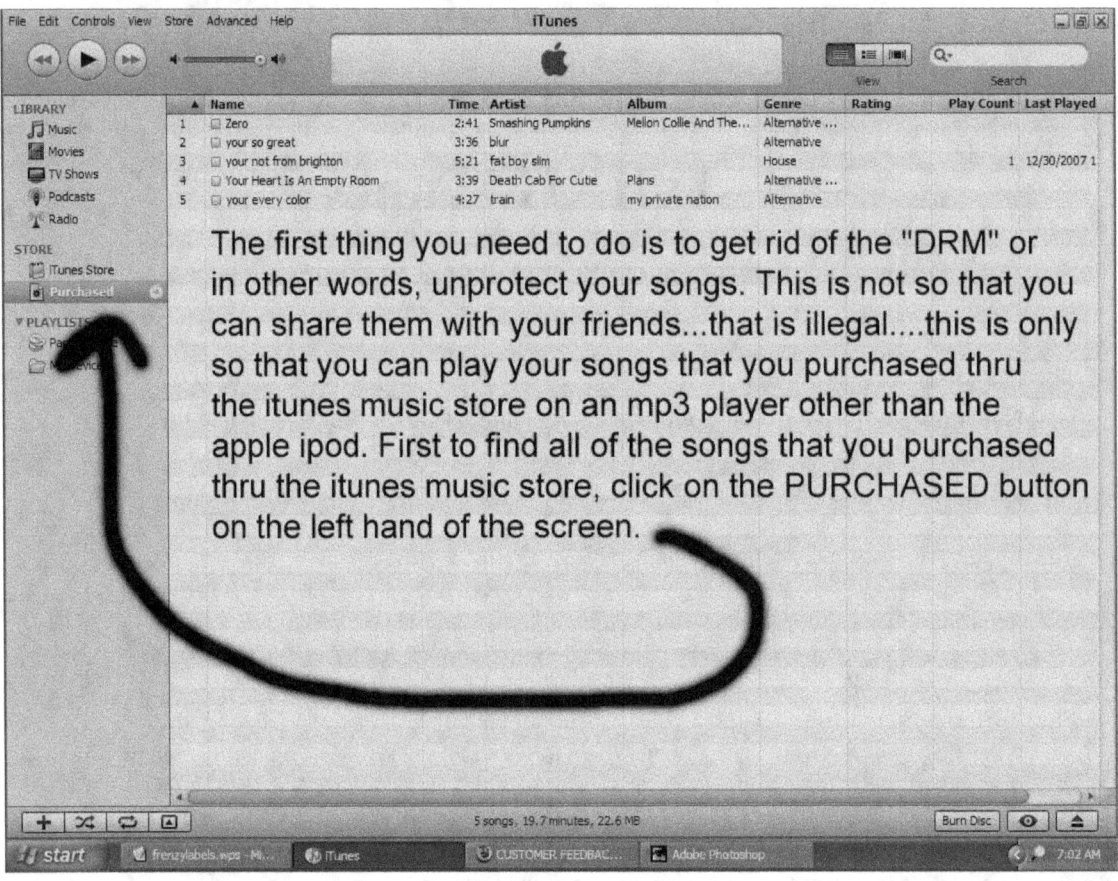

2. To highlight all of your songs, first click on the first song… then go to the last song on the list, hold down the "shift" key and click on the last song…this will highlight all of your songs… now you need to burn them to cd to get rid of the DRM… Put a blank cd in your burner and click "burn disk"

After you burn the protected AAC songs to disc you need to reload them… NOTE: You will now have two copies…one protected and one that is unprotected.

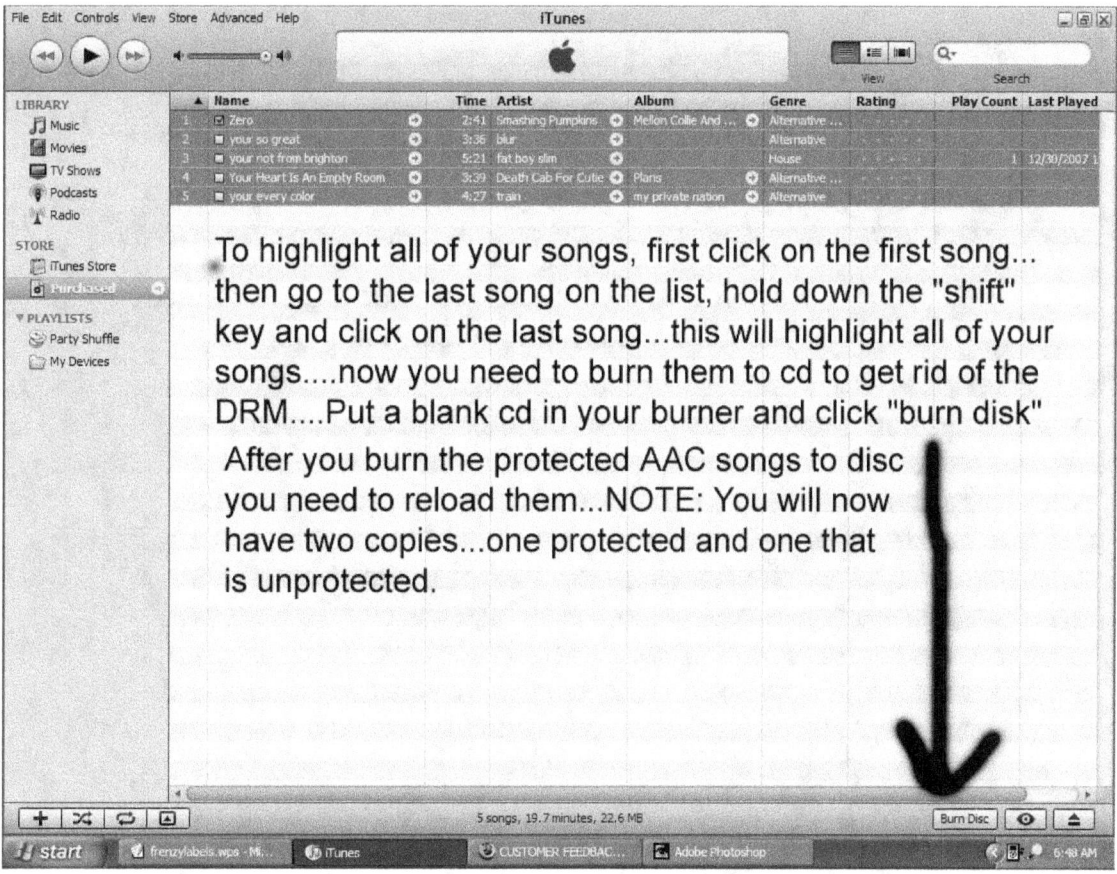

3.Now you will want to go to your MUSIC selection. Press the music button on the left menu.

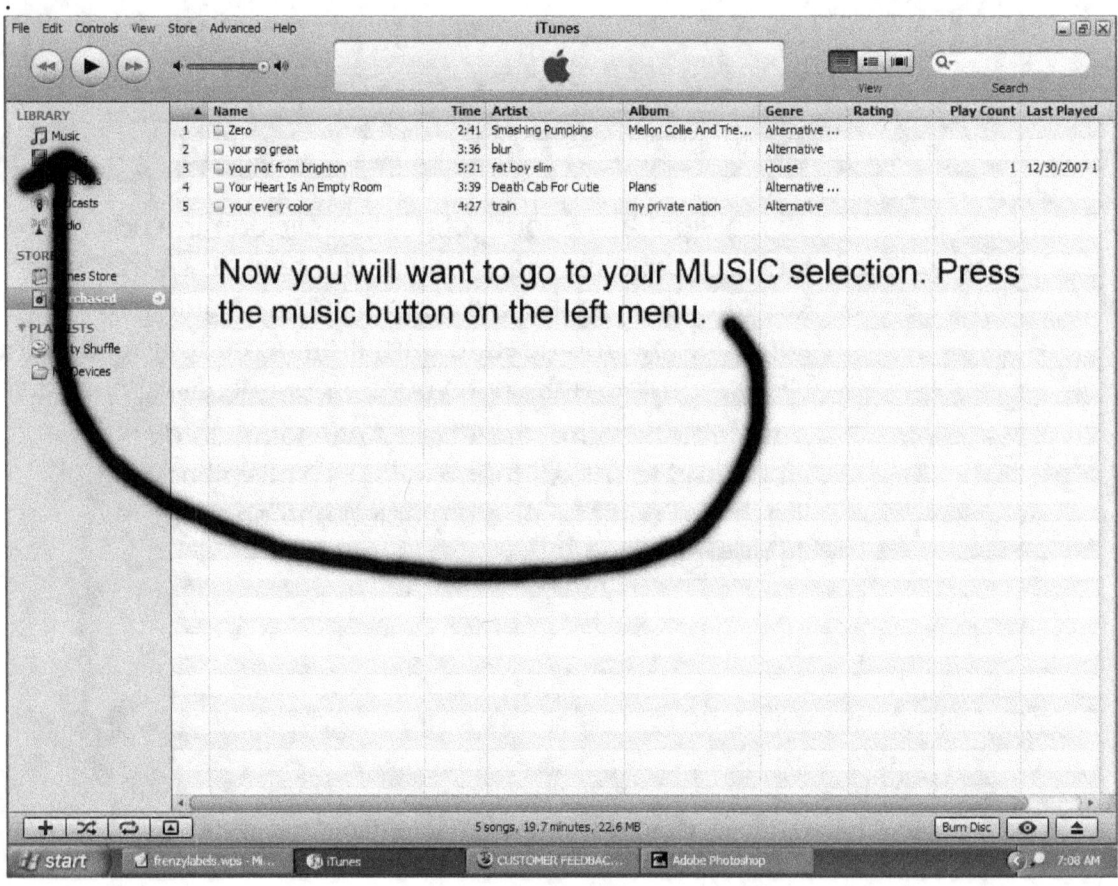

4. Again-highlight all of your songs…click on the first song…scroll to the last song…hold down the "shift" key and click on the last song… All of your songs are now highlighted blue as seen here!…. Now you will "right click" and select "convert selection to MP3" If you have over 2000 songs like myself this is going to take a while….so go out to eat, or go to bed! But first ensure that everything is working correctly.

5. If everything is working correctly you will see that it is converting…

Now when this is finIshed, you will have two copies of every song…. One in the AAC format which is only playable on apple ipod, and one in the MP3 format which is playable on apple ipod and basically every other mp3 player on the market! Including cell phones, e.t.c.

Now you have two options…either erase all of the files in Aac format… this may take a while… or if you are not particular on which software to use then stay tuned for further instructions.

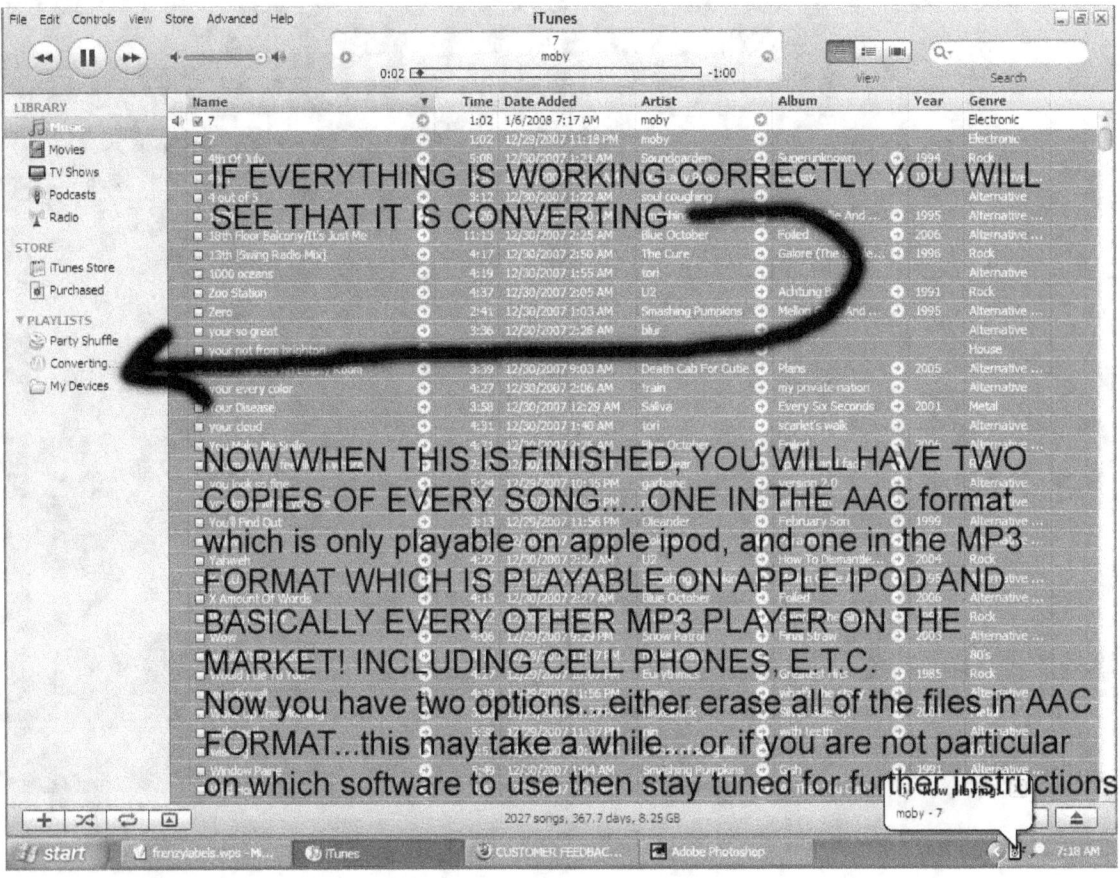

6. If you have decided that you really want to use itunes as your main software for loading music onto your mp3 player, then you will need to delete all the songs that are in AAC Format. Now itunes Default is to put all songs loaded into it, into the AAC Format… This means that if you load your personal CD's into itunes, It will automatically be converted into the AAC Format, unless you change the settings. To change the settings so that cd's loaded into itunes will be converted into the MP3 format (playable on most devices, including apple ipod) follow these directions… In the top right corner click edit, then select Preferences.

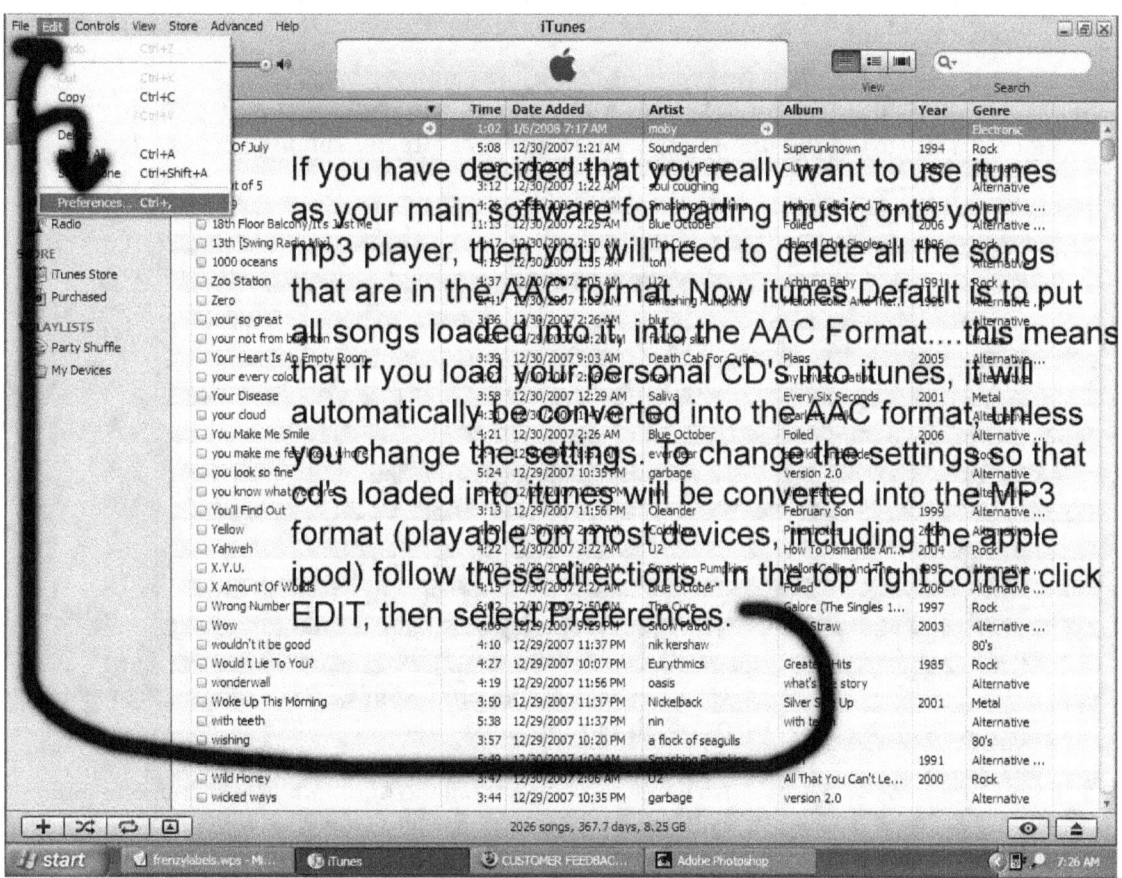

7.

1. Click on the "ADVANCED TAB"
2. Click on the "IMPORTING TAB"
3. Under "import using" Change to "MP3 ENCODER"

Now all songs loaded from your CD Collection into ituens will automatically be converted into the MP3 format.

Now that all songs are in the MP3 format you can load them onto your MP3 PLAYER using the itunes agent that you have already set up using our USER MANUAL.

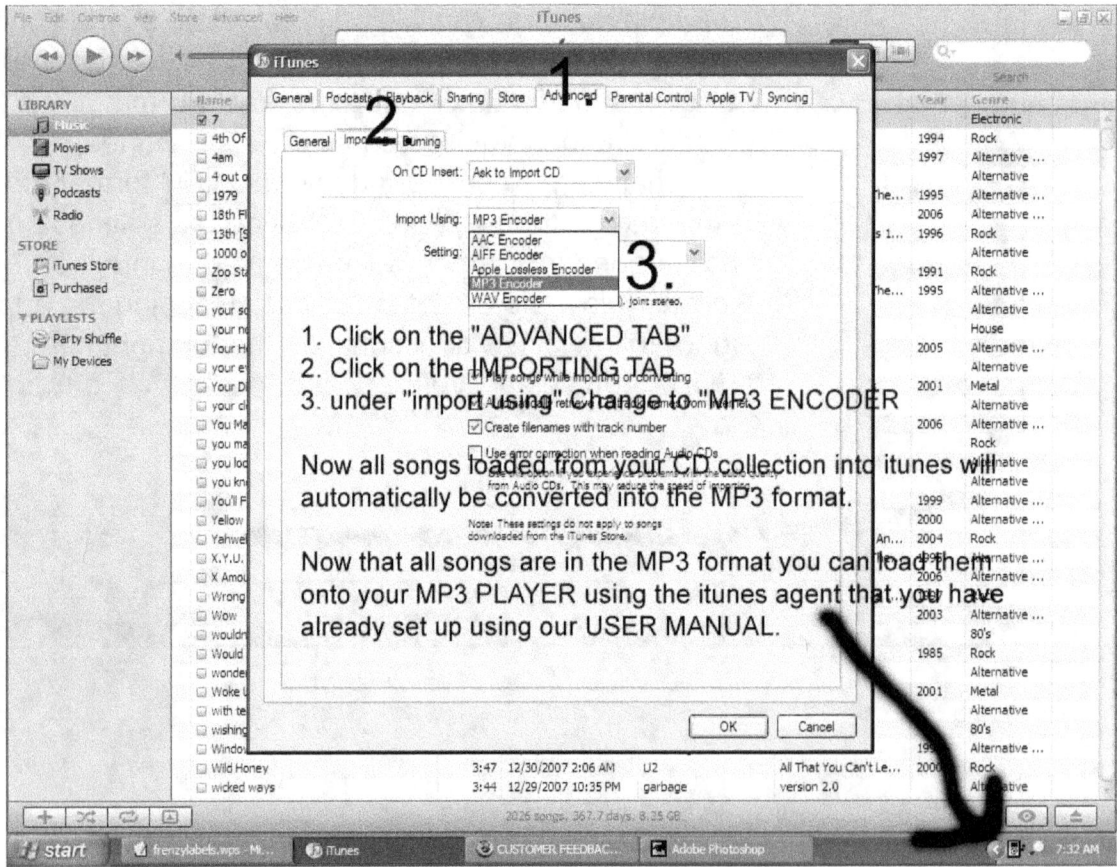

8. So if you are lazy like me and do not want to erase every other song on your itunes library, then open up windows media player 11…

1. Click on the library tab
2. Click "add to library"

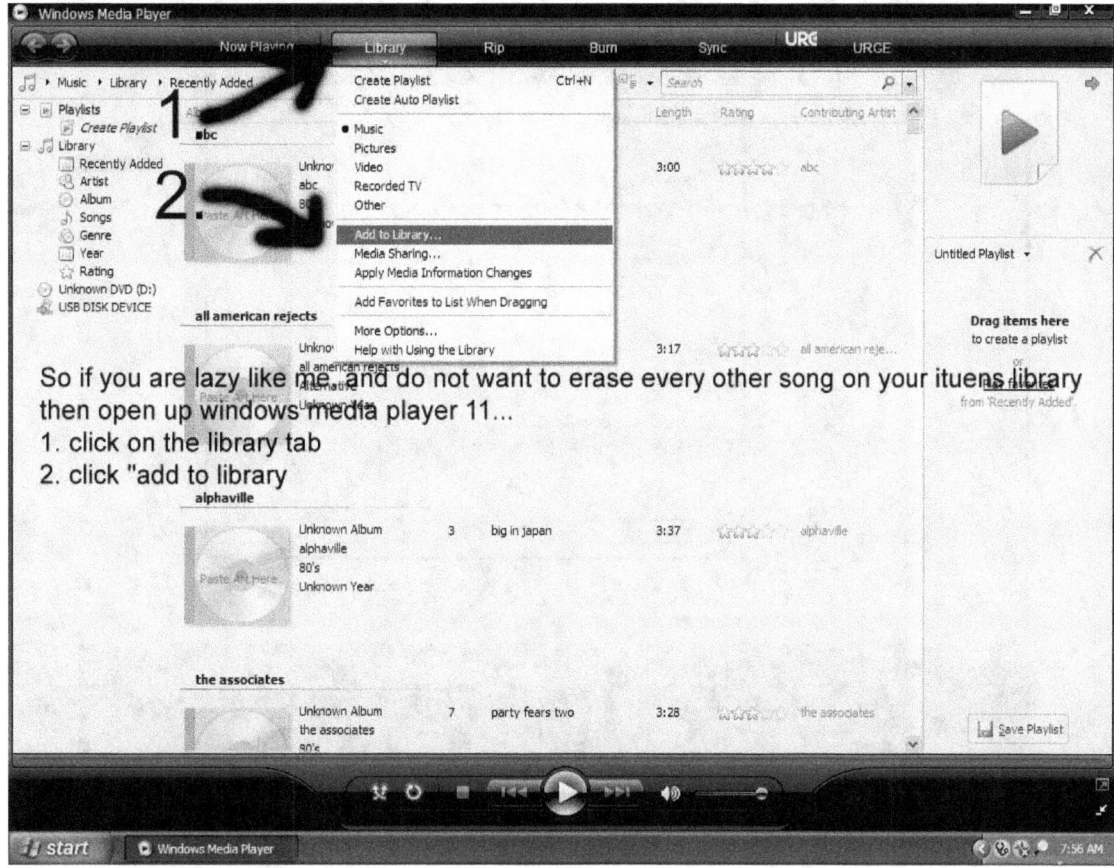

So if you are lazy like me, and do not want to erase every other song on your ituens library then open up windows media player 11…
1. click on the library tab
2. click "add to library

9. Now select the folder where your itunes music is stored…it is usually found in "my documents" My Music…itunes… select ADD then OK

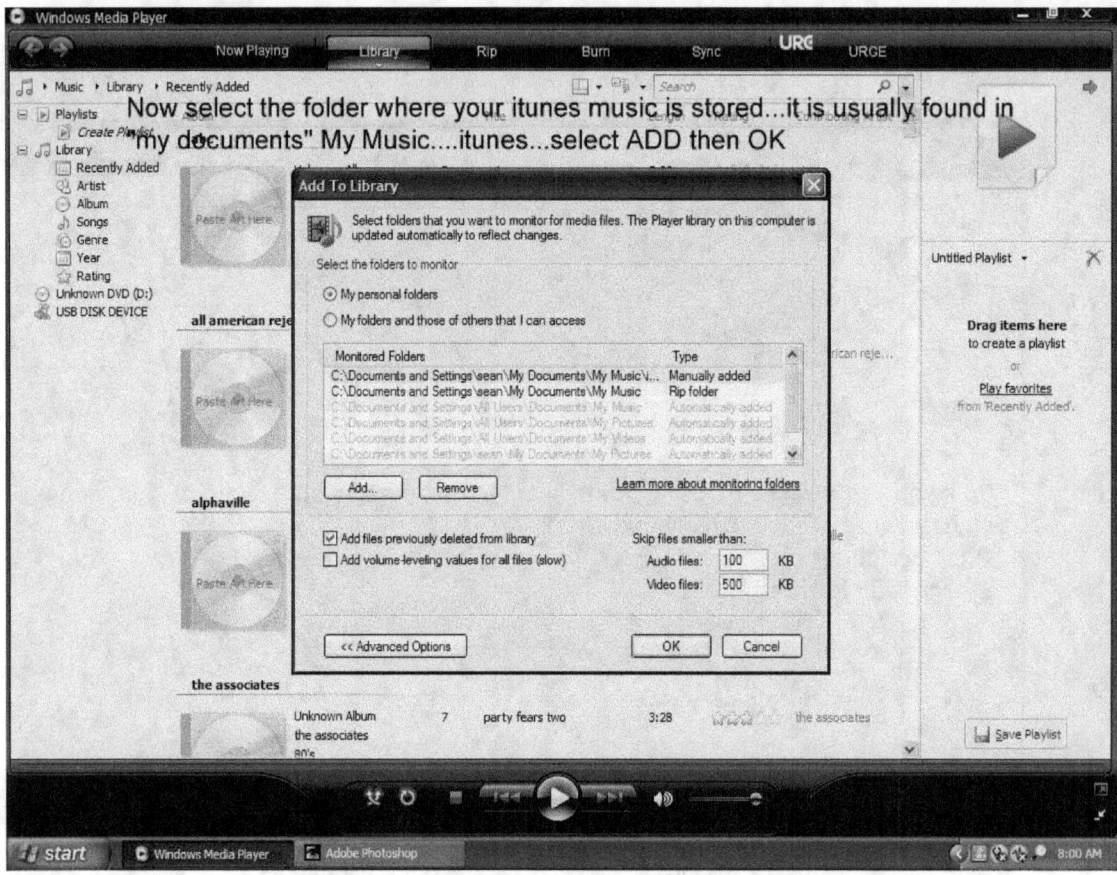

MOVIE / VIDEO

PLAY MOVIE / VIDEO – FROM MAIN MENU Scroll over to MOVIE in MAIN MENU, press MENU to select.

The MOVIE will be paused.

PLAY MOVIE - Press the CENTER PLAY/PAUSE button to play the movie.

FF/RW – PRESS and HOLD FF or RW Button.

NEXT CLIP/PREVIOUS CLIP – Press FF/RW button.

VOLUME – Press the VOLUME button, then press FF/VOL+ or RW/VOL- button to adjust volume accordingly.

RETURN TO MAIN MENU – PRESS and HOLD "MENU" Button.

DOWNLOAD MOVIE/VIDEO TO YOUR MEDIA PLAYER-

To play MP4 and other video files you have to convert them to the AMV format

Please click on the link below, if you have not already downloaded AMV 4.0

http://www.frenzygear.com/thankyou.htm

To use the AMV Convert Tool, please make sure you have installed:

1)   Windows Media Player 9 or above.

http://www.microsoft.com/windows/windowsmedia/player/downlo
ad/download.aspx

2)   Microsoft DirectX 9.0 or above –

http://www.microsoft.com/downloads/details.aspx?FamilyId=2DA43D38-
DB71-4C1B-BC6A-9B6652CD92A3&displaylang=en

To use the AMV CONVERTER 4.0 the original file format must be in the .AVI or .WMV format before converting
to .AMV which is the only format that will play on your device… If you file is not in .AVI or .WMV you must convert
it to .AVI or .AMV before converting to .AMV

Here is a list of software that will convert your files into .AVI or .WMV so that you can convert them into .AMV

Auto Gordian Knot
(This is a program that you can download to your computer for converting all types
of files to .AVI so that they can be converter to .AMV)

http://www.autogk.me.uk/index.php?name=Downloads&d_op=viewdownload&cid=1

For help using Auto Gordian Knot visit the following website.

http://www.autogk.me.uk/modules.php?name=TutorialEN

_Visit Zamzar.com
(This tool converts your file online and emails it to you for free!)

http://zamzar.com/url/

(If you use zamzar to convert your files online then you do not need to download
Auto Gordian Knot, or the FLV Converter)

Just remember, whatever you are converting, you must first convert the file to .AVI then you can use the AMV Converter for the final conversion._

After files have been converter to .AVI or .WMV you are ready to convert the files into .AMV

Let's try it!

Install AMV CONVERTER 4.0 to your computer.

The Converter will appear.

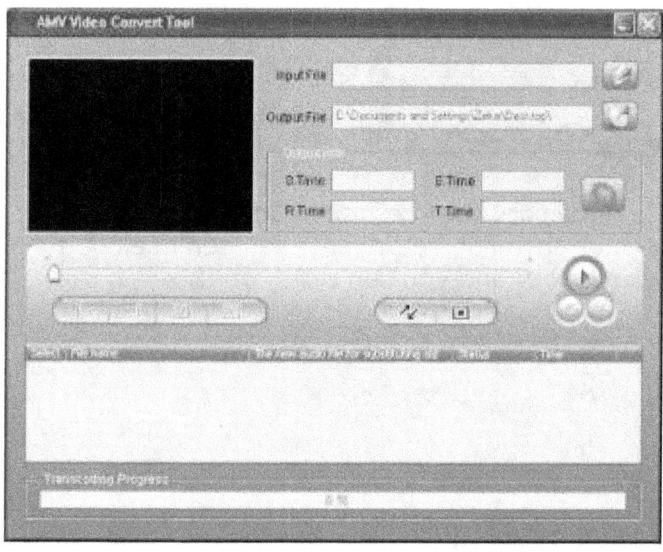

INPUT FILE: Click on the FILE ICON in the upper right corner to find the video file you would like to convert.

OUTPUT FILE: Click on the CD/DVD symbol. Find MY COMPUTER and CLICK ON IT. Select the Drive your MP3 PLAYER is connected to. Then Click on the MOVIE FOLDER.

(If you do not have a MOVIE folder on your media device, you can create one by opening it up and creating a NEW FOLDER and name it MOVIE.)

(If you do not see your device- unplug it from the USB PORT, turn the device OFF, wait a second…now TURN IN BACK ON…while it is coming back on PLUG IT BACK IN to the USB PORT…) IF THIS DOES NOT WORK, THEN CLOSE OUT THE AMV CONVERTER…FOLLOW THE DIRECTIONS ABOVE, THEN OPEN UP THE AMV CONVERTER AGAIN.

Select the file you want to encode in the queue list below.

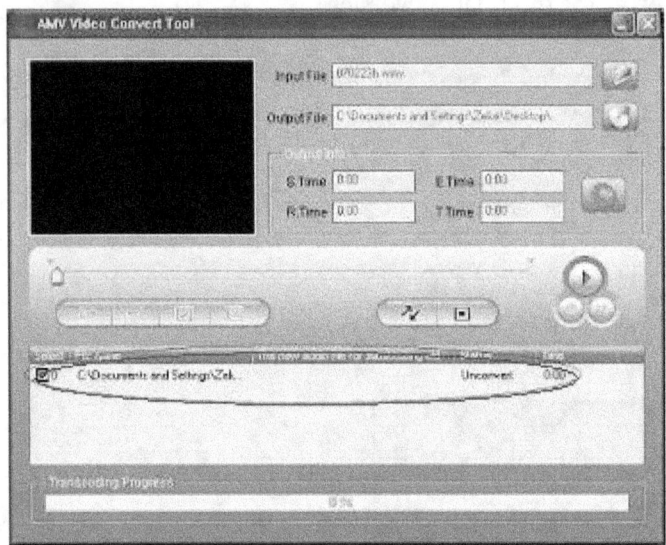

Highlight the file by clicking on the file name. Then press the [**Settings**] button on the right hand side to change your encoding settings. If you don't select the file, the [Settings] button is greyed out and you can't click on it.

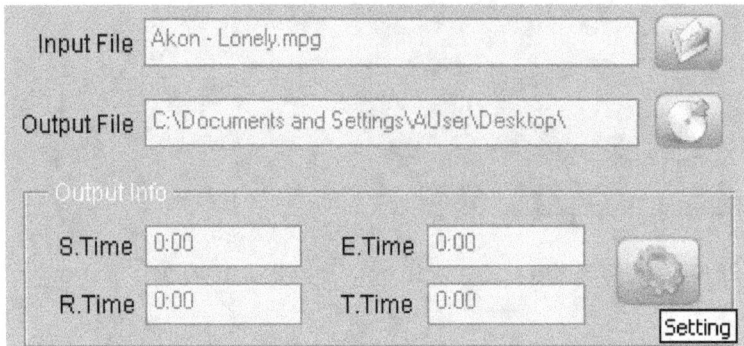

Output file: J:/FRENZY/Movie/ (Depending on your computer your device drive may be different, find the drive your MP3 PLAYER is connected to and direct the movie to be placed in the Movie folder…if you don't have a movie folder you can create one.)

For "**screen width and height**", change it to "160x120" if you have a 1.8″ screen player. "128x96" if you have a 1.5" screen player.

Make sure "Frames per second" and "image quality" is set to "**high**".
<u>NOTE:</u> If you have problems with 'Format Error" messages during playback on your player, change the "image quality" to "**medium**" instead.

Tick "**Try another codec**" if you have errors trying to encode a video to .AMV, this might fix it.

Click on [**OK**] button.

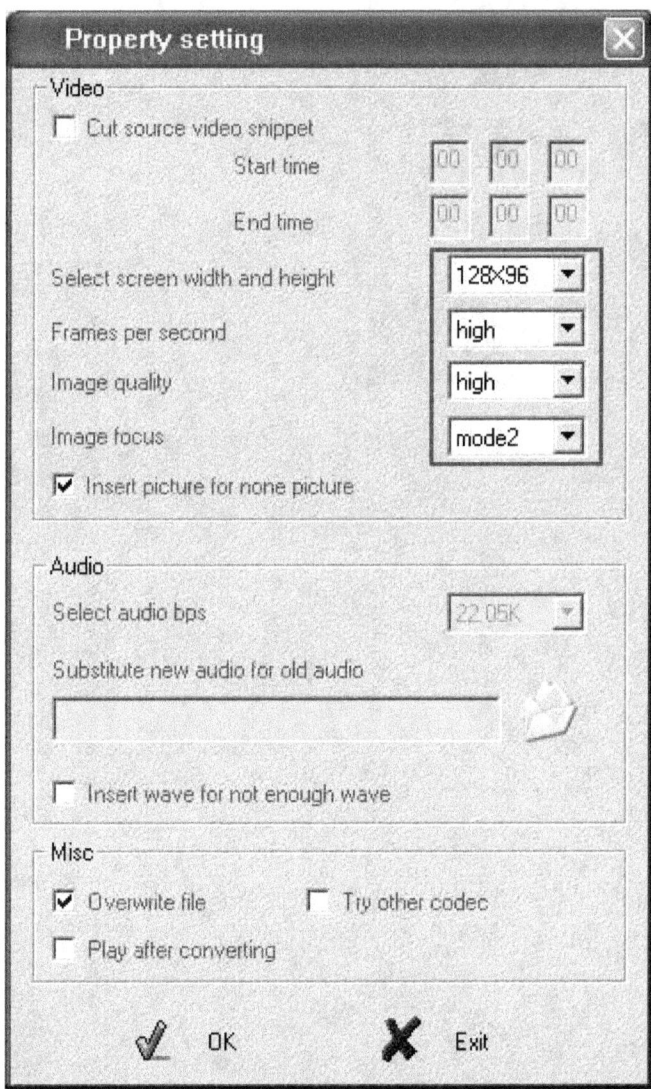

Click on the convert button and the file will start converting. The Transcoding Progress box will start to change color and the 0% will increase indicating how much of the file is done.

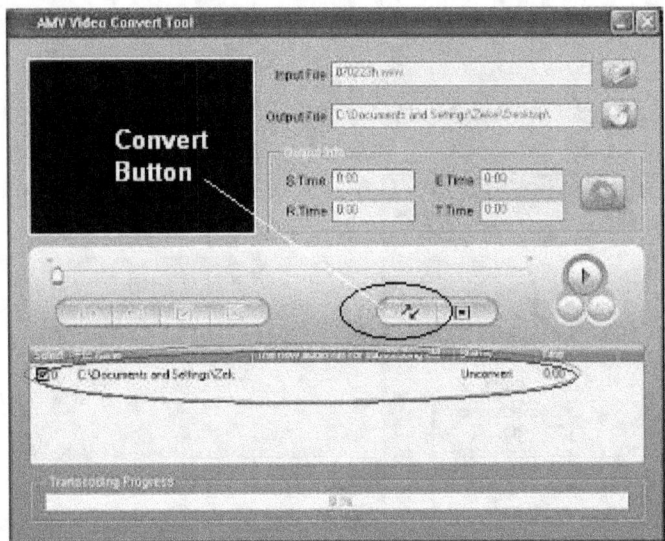

When the conversion is complete the new AMV file will start playing automatically in the AMV Player.

Close the AMV Player if you don't want to watch it on your PC.

VOICE RECORD

VOICE RECORD – FROM MAIN MENU Scroll over to RECORD in MAIN MENU, press MENU to select.

The VOICE RECORDER will be paused.

START RECORDING - Press the CENTER PLAY/PAUSE button to START RECORDING

PAUSE RECORDING – Press Center PLAY/PAUSE BUTTON.

RESUME RECORDING FROM PAUSE MODE- Press the CENTER button again.

STOP RECORDING/SAVE FILE – Press Center PLAY/PAUSE BUTTON to STOP RECORDING. Then press MENU button to save the file. You will return to the MAIN MENU.

RETURN TO MAIN MENU – PRESS and HOLD "MENU" Button.

LISTEN TO YOUR VOICE RECORDINGS

FROM MAIN MENU Scroll over to VOICE in MAIN MENU, press MENU to select.

The RECORDING will be paused.

PLAY RECORDING - Press the CENTER PLAY/PAUSE button to play the FILE.

OR press the MENU button to access LOCAL FOLDER, or to DELETE MUSIC FILES.

FF/RW – PRESS and HOLD FF or RW Button.

NEXT RECORDING/PREVIOUS RECORDING – Press FF/RW button.

VOLUME – Press the VOLUME button, wait for the FLASHING SPEAKER at the top of the screen then press FF/VOL+ or RW/VOL- button to adjust volume accordingly.

To access REPEAT-EQUALIZER-TEMPO RATE-REPLAY

Press MENU button while RECORDING is PLAYING.

RETURN TO MAIN MENU – PRESS and HOLD "MENU" Button

FM RADIO

Important- Your headphones work like an antennae. If they are not plugged in then the radio will not be able to tune in to your favorite stations!

PLAY RADIO – FROM MAIN MENU Scroll over to RADIO in MAIN MENU, press MENU to select.

AUTO SEEK + SAVE – Use this if you want to save all the stations available to you.

Press the MENU button then scroll down to AUTO SEEK and press the MENU button again. The player will auto search and save all available stations.

SAVE YOUR FAVORITE STATION –Tune to your favorite station, Then press the MENU

BUTTON. Scroll to SAVE, then press the MENU BUTTON.

SWITCH between FAVORITE PRESET STATIONS – Press the CENTER button.

VOLUME – Press the VOLUME button, wait for the FLASHING SPEAKER at the top of the screen then press FF/VOL+ or RW/VOL- button to adjust volume accordingly.

RETURN TO MAIN MENU – PRESS and HOLD "MENU" Button.

PHOTO

UPLOAD PHOTOS – Select the photos you would like to put on your media player from your computer, then RIGHT CLICK on your mouse, select SEND TO, then select the Drive that your USB LINE is connected to. We recommend compressing your photo files for faster loading.

VIEW A SPECIFIC PHOTO – FROM MAIN MENU Scroll over to PHOTO in MAIN MENU, press MENU to select.

To view a specific photo use the arrow keys to highlight, then press the CENTER button to select.

SLIDE SHOW- FROM MAIN MENU Scroll over to PHOTO in MAIN MENU, press MENU to select, you will see a list of the photos you have available. Press MENU again. Use the arrow keys to select PLAY SET press MENU again. Use arrow keys to highlight AUTO PLAY press MENU then use ARROW KEYS to select time between photos 1-10 seconds. Press CENTER button again, you will see a list of your photos, use arrow keys to select where you would like to start then press the CENTER button again to START SLIDESHOW.

E-BOOK

Most EBOOKS are available in .pdf (adobe ebook reader),or .lit (Microsoft Reader)

All ebooks must be converted to .TXT format to be used with your MP4 player.

Microsoft Reader eBooks are formatted in Microsoft's proprietary "dot lit" format, so called because the file extension is .lit

We recommend using ABC Amber LIT Converter to convert your ebook to the .TXT format. Click on the link below to install it.

http://www.processtext.com/abclit.html

After the file has been converted to .TXT all you need to do is "right click" on the file, SEND TO: your MP4 PLAYER.

TROUBLE SHOOTING:

DISK ERROR- Reformat the device.

First, plug it into your computer.

Now on YOUR COMPUTER Click START/My Computer/ Right Click on the drive "FRENZY "

Now format the drive- Ensure to select FAT not FAT32 and perform a full format.

Now you can load your music e.t.c. on it…. (If you cannot locate FRENZY unplug it and plug it back in again)

DISK EMPTY- This is common when you perform a format. It will display this error until you have a least 1 song-video-photos-e.t.c.

BATTERY DOES NOT LAST AS LONG AS IT SHOULD- You may need to adjust the lcd settings.

1)   Turn Player on

2)   Use the arrow keys to find SET UP

3)   Press MENU to select SET UP

LCD set/DARKMODE-------- SET TO 30

Power off/ Off Time----------SET TO 0

SLEEP TIME -----------------------SET TO 0

SONG PLAYS FOR A FEW SECONDS, AND THEN GOES TO THE NEXT SONGS, WHICH ONLY PLAYS FOR A FEW SECONDS...

Most likely you have unintentionally selected to only play the "intro" to all songs...to change this...turn your mp4 player on..Scroll to MUSIC, press the MENU button, press the CENTER BUTTON, to start playing your music...(the music has to be playing to adjust this setting) While the music is playing, press the MENU button again...Select "REPEAT" by pressing the MENU button, select NORMAL to play each song in the order they are loaded onto your device...you can also choose from several other options...just don't select "intro" unless you want to continue only hearing the first few seconds of each song.

QUESTIONS AND ANSWERS:

If you have any questions please email me at feedingfrenzygear@msn.com and I will try to answer your questions as quickly as possible. Thanks.

Q: **I got the manual, thanks. Just a few questions, seems I don't have much control in playing the musics. I'm trying to play one song from each folder, Have about 15 folders now. Is that a mistake. Seems it can only play sequencially, even I have selected Random. Should I put all songs in one 'music' folders only, then select Random, Instead of creating a folder for each singer. How to convert karaok to play in the mp4 player. The converted file has the video, and music only, but missing the vocal. Looking forward to your reply**

A: These types of players are not very good for creating music playlists. Generally if you have under 50 songs you can scroll through your folders (Playlists) and pick the song you want. But if you go over about 50 then they usually bog down and return to the main menu. There is nothing that can be done about this as it is the chip inside. Personally I don't mind becuase I get tired of the same playlists, and even though these types of mp4 players play all of the songs sequentially they save where you left off so you don't always start off at the beginning and have to work your way through a few thousand songs depending on how many GB you have.

That is about the only downside to these players compared to the ipod nano, but unlike the ipod these types play radio and voice recording. I love the radio, you can tune in to the t.v.'s at the gym, and record your favorite radio shows.

As far as the karaoke I don't think there is anything that you can do about that, I mean you could convert the video/music to amv format and load it onto your mp4 player, but the vocal will not be there since it never was to begin with.

_Q_: _I received the manual, thank you. When I first received the MP4 I turned it on but did not yet have your manual. The battery showed a good charge but it has shut off and I cannot get it back on. Can you please help with this?_

A: It could be a few things... either it is toast, or your charger could be dead, or your usb line could be dead. Most likely it is either toast or your charger is dead. Have you tried plugging it into your computer? This would eliminate the charger. If that doesn't work then it is probably toast. But you could try buying another usb line. Also you may have a charger for a phone that would fit, make sure it has the same amount of pins though.